exceptional
TREEHOUSES

exceptional TREEHOUSES

ALAIN LAURENS, DANIEL DUFOUR, GHISLAIN ANDRÉ, and LA CABANE PERCHÉE
Photographs by JACQUES DELACROIX

Abrams, New York

One April morning, in front of the treehouse that we had just completed, a client said to me,

"You have reawakened my childhood dreams."

This man had started and built a very large company, but this little treehouse, perched high in the air, caused him to hold back a tear and doubtless relive his whole childhood.

Over the last nine years we have built more than two hundred treehouses, and each time we have connected with that sensitive wellspring of childhood. Remembering those Sundays of our youth when we built our treehouses with a little bit of string, to play, but also to hide, alone in the world, safe from everything, happy.

We have built our treehouses in every country in Europe, and will soon build in the United States, and perhaps Japan, where I know we will find there those very same children who have decided not to grow up.

Alain Laurens

1

The Wisdom of Plants

Around the oak's bole, steadfast as the mainmast of a
sailing ship, winds the staircase. A dancing spiral, to
take leave of the ground. Here you enter the kingdom
of the branches and of the imagination, which unfolds
with the wooden stair treads. It is a helical maze in which
daydreams vertiginously coil and climb the levels of the
branches. Your step becomes as light as air as you tread
to the heights near where the secret dialogue with the
heavens holds itself aloft.

A new alphabet to be forged, in harmony with our
dreams. Is that a treehouse or a crow's nest dwelling in
the canopy? There we can draw on the strength of the
trunk, that incredible self-possession that is the oak's most
distinctive feature. With a fairy tale bestiary for a neighbor,
thirty-five feet above the ground, you could spirit away a
bird's feather to write someone a letter.

REGION: Normandy, France
TREE: Oak
HEIGHT: 33 feet
TREEHOUSE: 100 square feet
TERRACE: 85 square feet

2.

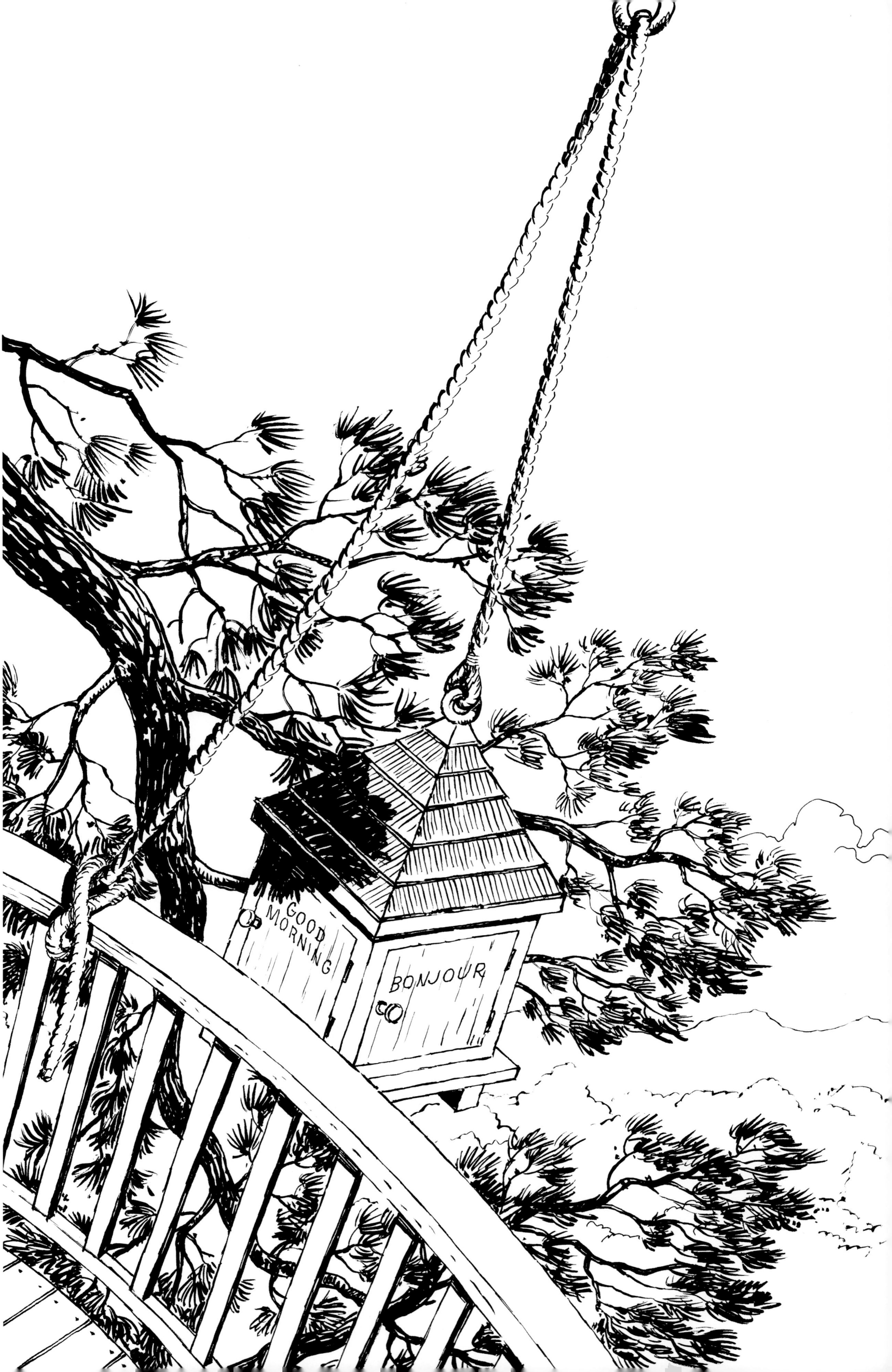

REGION: Luberon, France
TREE: Pine
HEIGHT: 17 feet
TREEHOUSE: 185 square feet
BATHROOM: 55 square feet
TERRACE: 95 square feet

Tales of the Canopy

Nestled in the foliage, the treehouse watches over our dreams. The spacious bed opens onto murmuring trees who tell heroic tales of the squirrel and the woodpecker. On the deck the pine's furrowed bark keeps its secrets. There are great expanses of glass at the heart of the leaves, to clear the view. It's time to bathe in green. At night the treehouse turns into a torch, a luminous signal at the center of the great silence. Shall we turn off the lights?

3

Perched Secret

Some treehouses really look like roosts. In some ways a treehouse is similar to a wading bird, like a long-beaked heron clothed in wood, standing acrobatically on one leg.

Winter is the time when, stripped of its leaves, the tree's birdlike form is most clearly revealed. After ascending the staircase, you reach the nest, tucked amid the branches.

Do the leaves transform the treehouse into a roost? Or is it the child's imagination, nourished by the tree? The fact that the child is an adult makes not the slightest difference.

REGION: Near Paris, France
TREE: Oak
HEIGHT: 36 feet
TREEHOUSE: 100 square feet
TERRACE: 75 square feet

4.

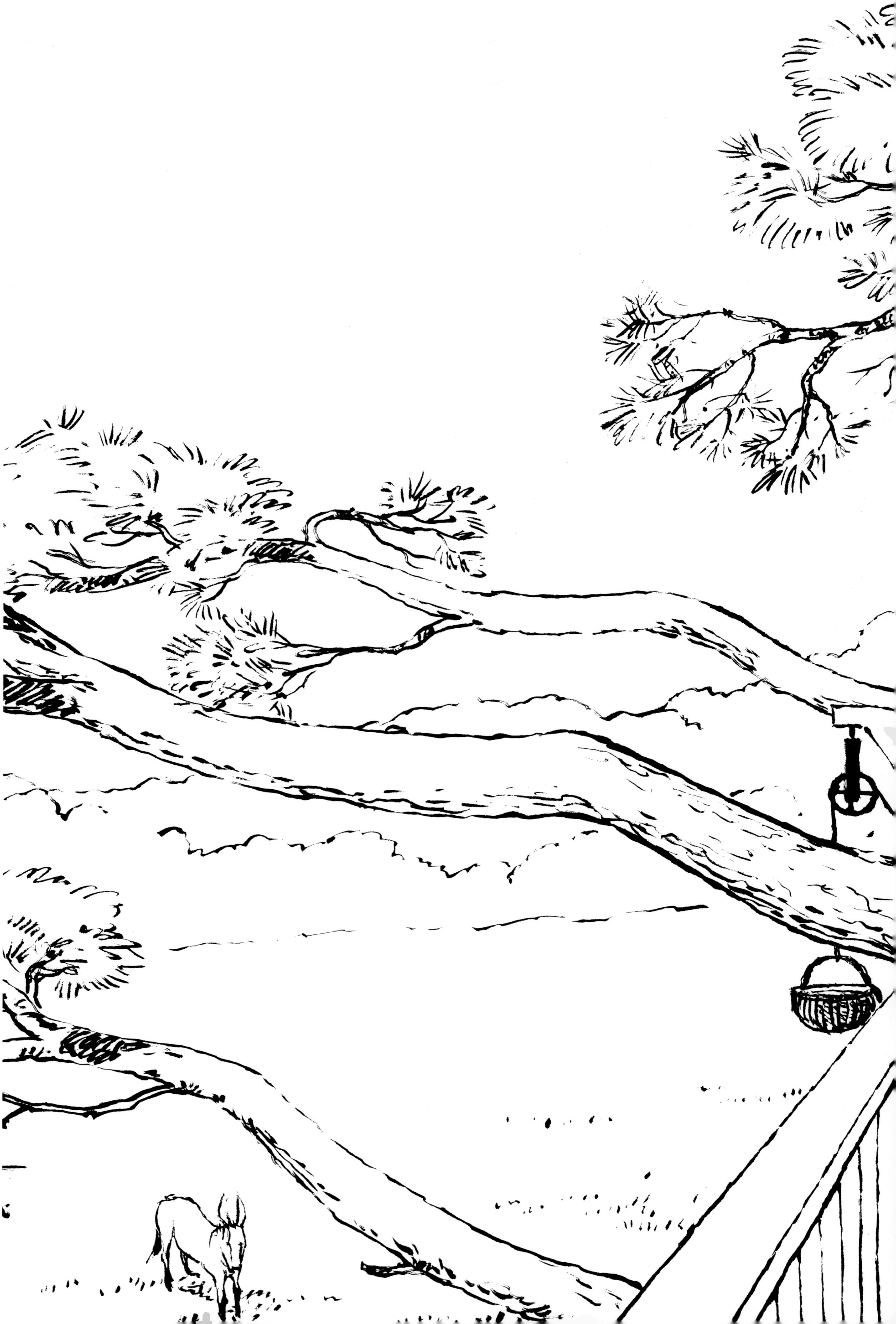

Beauty with a Parasol

Stone pines are easily recognized by their distinctive arching crowns. They always tilt their parasols slightly, a charming trait typical of these insouciant beauties. The bark? With its crevices of red ocher, it is as dizzying as the Grand Canyon! At the tree's base, your fingers search for the pine nuts between the scales of its cones. Nibbler's report: Victory! The little nuts have no wings with which to flee. In the middle of the vertigo, the treehouse stands. Stasis apart from the world, a quiet stage under the great green cumulonimbus clouds. At that height, the spindly cypress seems less haughty. And the surrounding olive trees sparkle like fanciful progeny. The waning daylight soaks the western side of the treehouse and the nearby branches in golden light. Which lends its color to the other? The treehouse, a perfect chameleon, sits silently within the murmuring branches.

And so, from now on, here it is at home.

REGION: Near Nice, France
TREE: Pine
HEIGHT: 36 feet
TREEHOUSE: 120 square feet
TERRACE: 75 square feet

5

The Epic Treehouse

A linden tree stood next to a castle filled to the brim with stories of knights, of fairies with long gowns, and with whinnying horses. And just think, the memory of a linden tree may reach back a thousand years. It too wanted to experience an epic moment. It was bedizened with a treehouse. From then on the linden tree gathered so many stories that it had to write the *Tales of the Perched Treehouse*. You can almost hear the twittering children: "Did it ever see a unicorn?"

REGION: Dordogne, France
TREE: Linden
HEIGHT: 23 feet
TREEHOUSE: 75 square feet
TERRACE: 160 square feet

6.

Echo Stop

Why do treehouses always seem to be keeping a secret? The staircase turns like a snake, as if winding around an enigma. Perhaps it takes the time to reflect, to take the pulse of that immense life force that lies within the trunk. The forest, after all, is nothing but the infinite repetition of the letter *l*. The steps of the staircase embrace the trunk in narrow circles, a wedding dance to enchant the bole with love without smothering it. Similarly, the treehouse will grow without ever necessitating the death of a single branch in its construction. And suddenly we understand that long ascent along the bark. The treehouse revolves around the tree, like a dance partner, the way the tree rings grow as they patiently form the trunk.

REGION: Rambouillet Forest, France
TREE: Oak
HEIGHT: 46 feet
TREEHOUSE: 65 square feet
TERRACE: 85 square feet

The Bride and the Pollard

A staircase? Or is it really the wooden train of the great oak's wedding dress falling to the ground? Could it be a new root added by the hand of man? This tree has style! In arboreal language, it's called a pollard. It is not at all the same thing as a dullard. Pollard is the name for stocky oaks, those old trees that stand alone in the meadows. These trees are maintained by the hand of man, in this case a pruner, and are kept with a short trunk and shoots at the crown to facilitate periodic trimming. The thick planks run through the treehouse like veins. It is a colossal oak, bound to play a starring role. The one everyone admires through the window, the one that attracts all the birds. It is the rugged type, well built, with a swimmer's shoulders, reminiscent of a young Marlon Brando. The oak has a sweeping crown, with leaves that almost caress the ground. At its breast, a treehouse—the betrothed—whom it seems to shield from view. Because in the oak's memory, it didn't always have a treehouse.

49

REGION: Italy
TREE: Oak
HEIGHT: 20 feet
TREEHOUSE: 185 square feet
BATHROOM: 45 square feet
TERRACE: 150 square feet

8

The Treehouse at the End of the Road

Up above, on the path through the branches, right at the end of the road in the trees there is a treehouse. Perched in plain sight. Upright. Suspended in the void, holding on by magic, and supported by slender, graceful wooden stilts. The treehouse almost seems to have a sense of humor, a sort of bravado with respect to the laws of gravity, thumbing its nose at the serious side of life. It looks like a hut on a patch of green sand. Caressed by the sea of clouds. Floating in that ocean of jade, the red cedar takes on the hues of the setting sun. It's the treehouse at the end of… Complete the sentence for yourself.

REGION: Near Lyon, France
TREE: Oak
HEIGHT: 20 feet
TREEHOUSE: 65 square feet
TERRACE: 65 square feet

9.

Finery

It is autumn. The great oak, in consultation with its
colleagues of the forest, has decided that it is time to let
fall its leaves, but before the divestiture, a blaze of glory.
And now the treehouse's deck is flushed with the hues of
maple syrup: yellow-golds, reds, and oranges. Soon winter
will come, and the treehouse will no longer be able to hide
behind the foliage, revealing its graft and its audacious
embrace. It is an organic connection that unites the cabin
to the tree without the support of even a single nail. No
metal prostheses. It is a secret osmosis between the tree
and the house—an homage to wood, the strong binder
of the two.

REGION: Normandy, France
TREE: Oak
HEIGHT: 20 feet
TREEHOUSE: 120 square feet
BATHROOM: 45 square feet
TERRACE: 140 square feet

10.

Fillip

The treehouse is like a nest perched in the trees; an observatory from which you can view the beauty of the plains that stretch out below you as the deck seems to move forward like the bold prow of a ship. After the long climb up to the top of the treehouse, the pulley hauling up a basket with refreshments is a welcome sight—after all, contemplation doesn't satisfy the appetite!

REGION: Normandy, France
TREE: Oak
HEIGHT: 16 feet
TREEHOUSE: 100 square feet
TERRACE: 130 square feet

11.

Cotton Candy Trap

In my perfect seclusion—a space between heaven and earth—I heard the rumbling of the coming evening. Not one of those long speeches, empty as a hollow log, the destiny of every tree! But rather a ritual, almost intuited rather than heard. The walnut's crown of branches is abundant and dense, almost vaporous, looking like a clump of cotton candy. A chameleon cotton candy that has turned from pink to green and looks like it spends its time trapping the clouds amid the tracery of the leaves.

The treehouse is the heavens' floor, and on that floor I waited all day to see a big cloud ensnared in the branches' trap. To finally learn what the sky tastes like.

REGION: Provence, France
TREE: Walnut
HEIGHT: 20 feet
TREEHOUSE: 60 square feet
TERRACE: 130 square feet

12

The Green Sentinel

A tree is rooted in the ground, but its leaves are part of the sky's tapestry. The tree soars and flourishes with its crown of emerald fingers through which the random blue of the sky flashes. Wrapped in a woolen plaid blanket, feeling like a proud emperor of the world, surveying your land from above, perched in your treehouse. You keep watch for the mushrooms to tip their caps. Acting as a sentinel in the oak, how can you forget the words of Italo Calvino? "From the tree, Cosimo looked at the world; everything seen from up there was different...." (Italo Calvino, *The Baron in the Trees,* trans. Archibald Colquhoun [New York: Harcourt Brace Jovanovich, 1977] 13, 142).

REGION: Var, France
TREE: Oak
HEIGHT: 30 feet
TREEHOUSE: 75 square feet
TERRACE: 65 square feet

13

The Life of Objects at Altitude

We're off! Up the staircase that leads to our dreams. The hypnotic ascension feels like a fairy tale, like Jack and the Beanstalk, but without the giant.

The treehouse provides the perfect place to sleep among the leaves. A basket is used to haul up the lemonade, unless it's a little sparkling wine you prefer with your fresh porcini mushrooms, sliced thin and drizzled with olive oil. There, above everything, we take in the beauty of the heights. Our favorite books, wedged against the wood's knots, patiently await us.

At thirty feet above the ground, you can no longer believe in the life of objects. A marionette, made of linden wood told me so.

REGION: Provence, France
TREE: Oak
HEIGHT: 16 feet
TREEHOUSE: 100 square feet
TERRACE: 100 square feet

14

Time Difference

This enchanting hut is built in the tradition of Asian pagodas; latticework, bamboo, a little tiled roof, and above all, the spike that points to the sky. It is the perfect place for you to meditate and talk to the heavens. Through the latticework walls we can see the surrounding foliage imitate the colors of Japanese tea, and we feel like we've been swallowed up by the greenery. Relaxing among the cushions embroidered with flaming peonies, steeping tea in the cast-iron teapot, and admiring the bamboo plantation, you feel as though you've been transported to Kyoto.

REGION: Provence, France
TREEHOUSE: 85 square feet
TERRACE: 65 square feet

15

REGION: Normandy, France
TREE: Oak
HEIGHT: 33 feet
TREEHOUSE: 110 square feet
TERRACE: 75 square feet

A Holiday Feeling

The trunk stands tall like a flagpole, and at the very top rests the treehouse. This great oak is a classic specimen, standing proud in the clearing. The oak is a tree of boundaries, voluntarily solitary; and English oaks often seek the light at the edge of a clearing. The filtered rays of sunlight shine through the canopy, creating a cathedral-like stillness.

The staircase that wraps around the tree imitates its life force like an elongated furl of wood. From the distance, the staircase resembles a DNA molecule spiraling around the trunk.

16

The Jade Cabin

First, you see the beautiful expanse of water, and then floating on the calm surface of the pond, the Jade Cabin. But the beauty of the surroundings is born of the perfect fusion of water and sky. The roof of the cabin stands apart from the horizon; its verdigris tones will never blend into the foliage.

This cabin is man's response to nature, not its imitation. It embodies the soul of a teahouse. The pond plays the part of the *roji* ("dewy garden path") in the Japanese garden and leads to detachment. The mind, in its slow progress, can finally discard its worn-out, workday habits. Only then can you enjoy the simplicity of things, like a cup of *matcha* green tea, in which the bamboo whisk creates jade foam.

The essential restraint of the Jade Cabin, surrounded by water, restores the purity of human emotions. It is also called House of the Void, because it allows you to become aware of the ephemeral quality of life. According to Japanese tradition, no more than five persons are allowed inside: "More than the Graces, and fewer than the Muses," says Okakura Kakuzō. Here we learn that poetry is simple nourishment, because it goes back to the heart.

REGION: Eure-et-Loir, France
TREEHOUSE: 240 square feet
TERRACE: 830 square feet

17

Ocean View

The forest grows up through the treehouse as if it had always been there. The branches appear to have grown through the floorboards without resistance. Here the woven tree trunks, the tree's vertebral column, inspired the construction of the tree house. Stairways and railings grow out of the treehouse like rows of dominos. The treehouse looks like a little trawler with the deck's bow moving through the network of the foliage. Tell me, from up there, can you see the sea?

REGION: Provence, France
TREE: Oak
HEIGHT: 20 feet
TREEHOUSE: 120 square feet
TERRACE: 140 square feet

18

And in the Middle a Treehouse Stands

At first you don't see the treehouse, but you can sense it. Within the regular rhythm of the trunks that make up the forest, you can spot the terrace, whose narrowness is part of the treehouse's simplicity. To cross the bridge you have to leave gravity behind; we, too, have to get rid of some deadwood.

Now we are ready for contemplation: Was that a Tancho Kohaku koi that just swam by? White, with a single red circle on its head, which makes it look like the Japanese flag. The rustling of the woods sounds like the wings of an escaping bird. The treehouse, with its sliding wooden panels, opens like a lacquered pencil box. Sitting on the bed, where the sunlight filters through the leaves, you are so bathed in green that it's hard to believe you're inside. The treehouse allows nature to enter, as if the boundaries dissolved. The secret unfolds and we oscillate between the poles of Zen: the vitality of *wabi* ("simplicity") and the principle of *jaku* ("serenity").

REGION: Normandy, France
TREE: Pine
HEIGHT: 10 feet
TREEHOUSE: 120 square feet
TERRACE: 65 square feet

19

The Gaiety of Tendrils

The staircase winds around the treehouse and unfurls like a birthday ribbon that had been curled by scissors into a corkscrew. Looking at the treehouse, you can't help but think that the carpenter delighted in creating a long ribbon of wood that drops to the deck below, inviting you to come up. Next to the treehouse, deck chairs welcome the sun, which never misses an opportunity to linger overhead for a little while. Every day the sun passes by, like an old faithful friend. Sometimes just for five minutes, but today, by getting him to talk, we were able to keep him around for several hours. Just in time for the birthday party.

REGION: Sologne, France
TREE: Oak
HEIGHT: 26 feet
TREEHOUSE: 85 square feet
TERRACE: 130 square feet

20

The Knight of Modern Times

Look up—up to the lookout covered in green shoots. Hovering between heaven and earth, the shelter soars high above the ground. Here, you pause and reflect between the diviner and the divine. The pines seem to happily chirp in the sunlight. A poet once addressed a prayer "to the trees which, without the wind, would be silent as the tomb." [Jules Supervielle, Prière á l'inconnu]

A tree, silent? This poet didn't have this perch from which to listen to the song of the bark—for the trees do sing! They're regular chatterboxes, even in the middle of the night. You'd think you were surrounded by a band of squirrels, all rattling their walnut shells. A night in the treehouse really raises one's heroism quotient! The next morning, you awake and wink knowingly at the holm oak (*Quercus ilex*) because you have triumphed over the spirits of the forest and the night.

REGION: Luberon, France
TREE: Pine
HEIGHT: 16 feet
TREEHOUSE: 195 square feet
TERRACE: 225 square feet

REGION: Dordogne, France
TREE: Linden tree
HEIGHT: 30 feet
TREEHOUSE: 75 square feet
TERRACE: 160 square feet

Sharing Dreams

A tree is a dream that takes root.

A treehouse is a dream that takes height.

A Floating Base

Dreaming up a treehouse requires a whole new way of thinking. You must uproot old habits, and ignore the norm and never set your sights too low. The imagination is full of echoes of the bird-man, of hot-air balloons, of childhood games, and of Italo Calvino's *The Baron in the Trees*—making us daydream of Calvino's monkey, who "could have left Rome and skipped from tree to tree until it reached Spain, without ever touching earth." The staircase up to the treehouse unfurls its red carpet of cedar, leading the way to the kingdom of the air. And what a lesson is learned!

Who else but the tree can boast of having its feet planted in the earth and its head in the clouds? Perhaps the adult who is bent on fulfilling his or her simple childhood dreams.

REGION: Near Paris, France
TREE: Beech
HEIGHT: 20 feet
TREEHOUSE: 85 square feet
TERRACE: 150 square feet

23.

Summit Dialogue

Winter trees, like bare candelabra, stripped of their lights—autumn,

Ramifications of arterioles that delineate, roots in the sky,

The treehouse: commotion of the wood of banisters and impetuous trunks

Like the crossing of steel, of antique swords,

The stairs make everyone

By the slow climb

Become a giant.

When I grow up, I want to be an oak.

REGION: Alpes-de-Haute-Provence, France
TREE: Oak
HEIGHT: 13 feet
TREEHOUSE: 100 square feet
TERRACE: 195 square feet

24

In the Kingdom of the Giants

The sequoias are giant like a dinosaur's leg and very red like ocher. Touching the trunk is like caressing the woody fibers of a coconut. The sequoia calls for hyperbole—it is the Victor Hugo of trees, the giant of the forest! Here the poet and the scientist are in agreement, the tallest tree, the *Sequoia sempervirens* (Hyperion, at 379.1 feet) would just fit under the second story of the Eiffel Tower. The giant redwood (*Sequoiadendron giganteum)* is a close second at 275 feet (shorter than the sequoia, but with a greater volume than even Hyperion). The spiral staircase is adorned with a luxurious green boa of foliage—worthy of the ostrich feathers of a Parisian review.

Does the giant hide an ogre? Like the story of the boa constrictor in *The Little Prince* that devours an elephant? If told as *The Roosting Treehouse*, this would be the story of the redwood that devoured a treehouse.

REGION: Burgundy, France
TREE: Sequoia
HEIGHT: 40 feet
TREEHOUSE: 85 square feet
TERRACE: 150 square feet

25

Howdah in the Forest

The word "branch" is derived from the Latin word *branca,* meaning "animal's paw." On the edge of the forest, this treehouse is supported by two great oak trunks. The treehouse stands firmly on two sturdy legs and the deck pushes its balcony forward into the forest, like an elephant carrying the treehouse on its back.

Or maybe the oaks are more like a dappled gray Percheron horse. The imagination flows freely, but this treehouse knows that it will always have a place nestled in the branches of the great oak.

Next door to the treehouse, bushy young birches stand tall, looking like herons, tall and slender. While the birches are elegant, they don't possess the elephantine majesty of the oak. A narrow footbridge leads to the third part of the branch of the tree, where a spiral staircase winds down to the ground. Ariel redistribution: triumph of the gossamer tread. The treehouse, an elephant's howdah, sits on the animal's back, except that the rich draperies embroidered with gold and precious stones have given way to the luxuriance of the leaves in honey and tiger's-eye.

REGION: Sologne, France
TREE: Oak
HEIGHT: 23 feet
TREEHOUSE: 75 square feet
TERRACE: 85 square feet

26

Stellar Dialect

The treehouse transforms its features with the four seasons. Whether it has lost its finery or is radiant with green, the tree remains beautiful.

Like an arboreal snake, the stairway drops down lovingly to the ground. Higher up, behind the windowpanes, the candlesticks look like trunks of wax. The flames that are neither moon nor sun flicker in the windows until the candles are snuffed out, and we go out to the deck to greet the stars, the candles' luminous rivals.

Treading softly on crumpled leaves on the forest floor, the stags and deer meet as night falls. Little by little our eyes grow accustomed to the half-light, and then the sky fully reveals its hieroglyphics. The gaze draws imaginary figures in the night sky and quickly picks out the constellations. The Summer Triangle connects Deneb in the constellation Cygnus, and Vega in Lyra and Altair in Aquila. Deneb is a stellar trinity at the end of the Milky Way, a blue supergiant, big as two hundred suns. Secured to the wooden railing, the dream spins its fabric, and one wonders if the treehouse can speak to the skies through the language of night.

REGION: Sologne, France
TREE: Oak
HEIGHT: 23 feet
TREEHOUSE: 100 square feet
TERRACE: 130 square feet

27

Under the Stars

The monumental beech has grown patiently, only a half-inch to an inch per year. In autumn it hatched a treehouse that looks like a wading bird perched in her branches. Traveling across the treehouse's footbridge, one is reminded of the skillful balancing talent of a tightrope walker. Under the tent of the heavens, the treehouse sleeps under the stars.

REGION: Champagne, France
TREE: Beech
HEIGHT: 30 feet
TREEHOUSE: 120 square feet
BATHROOM: 45 square feet
TERRACE: 45 square feet

28

The Lighthouse of the Cypress

In the beautiful mosaic of blue and green foliage, a giant cypress; it stands out against the countryside. Under the arched crown of the great cypress nestles a vessel that will never return to the waves. As the mind wanders, we find ourselves at the confluence of ocean, earth, and sky. The perched pavilion looks like a motionless ocean liner.

Tucked safely behind the porthole of the door, writing letters at the simple desk, you're not afraid to hear the wind howl because you feel secure in your cabin in the trees. On the deck you pick up a cone that has opened its scales, offering the cypress's small seeds. Up close, the cone looks like a *Rosa centifolia*, a cabbage rose; it is more like a petrified rose that smells of turpentine. The green anise cones of the cypress tree look like miniature art deco roses made from sugar.

At night the slow metamorphosis comes, transforming the cabin from ocean liner to lighthouse.

REGION: Brittany, France
TREE: Cypress
HEIGHT: 43 feet
TREEHOUSE: 140 square feet
TERRACE: 90 square feet

29

Cabin on the Water

The Cabin on the Water was designed by La Cabane Perchée to serve as a tranquil place situated on a body of water like a pond or lake, to escape to. Built of red cedar, it offers a level of comfort that allows you to think only of the pleasures of living in the middle of nowhere. Here you can let yourself go, and fall asleep, cradled by the lapping water.

TREEHOUSE: 190 square feet
TERRACE: 285 square feet

The Staff of
La Cabane Perchée

Alain
Laurens

Daniel
Dufour

Ghislain
André

Mayra
Da Silveira Beuno

Pierre
Nègre

www.lacabaneperchee.com
Alain Laurens + 33 4 90 75 91 40

Aimé
Baret

Matthieu
Adamski

Anna
Chevolleau

Antoine
Leib

Baptiste
Colliaux

Locations Where You Can Sleep in the Trees

FRANCE

Apt 84400
www.evasioninsolite.unblog.fr

Bellou-le-Trichard 61130
www.perchedansleperche.com

Bermicourt 69510
www.lacourderemi.com

Bonnieux 84480 / Page 13
www.maisonvalvert.com

Chigny les Roses 51500 / Page 171
www.domaine-du-chalet.com

La Croix Valmer 83420
www.chateauvalmer.com

Gommenec'h 22290
www.lesecuriesdekerbalan.com

Maubec 85660
www.hotel-bastide-bois-breant.com

Prats de Mollo 66230
www.montozarbres.com

Nomécourt 52300
www.chatnom.com

St Paul de Vence 06570
www.orionbb.com

Thurins 69150
www.cabanotte.fr

ITALY

Italie / Page 44
Arlena di Castro
www.lapiantata.it

Italie
Merano
www.hotel-irma.com

Acknowledgments

The authors wish to convey their warmest gratitude to all those who trusted them and sheltered them in the trees. In this way, they allowed us to pursue adventure.

Isabelle Grison and the whole team at Éditions de la Martinière, who fulfilled our every need.

Marion Laurens, talented artistic director for this book, whose nights and weekends we stole.

Magnus Keyser for the photograph on page 4.

Maurizio Brera for the photographs on pages 46–49.

The whole wonderful team who make up La Cabane Perchée. In all kinds of weather they built this book, and for this reason they are its principal authors.

Daniel Dufour's Sketches*

*Sample designs that we send to our clients

We never cut a large branch or drive a nail into a tree. Originally, because of a large branch that prevented our passage, the imposing spiral staircase was supposed to stop at a platform and extend toward the deck. We were able to get around the obstacle so the staircase extends to the deck directly without stopping at a landing.

This guesthouse is unique in that it rests simultaneously on pilings and on two large pine trees that pass through the deck. It has a bathroom in which the plumbing is completely concealed.

This was the first time we built a spiral staircase so far away from the trunk; we did so in order to avoid cutting any of this magnificent oak's branches. Because we had to build the staircase more than six feet from the trunk, we were inspired to make it entirely self-supporting. The intersection between the curved staircase and the straight part of the landing was difficult to carry out.

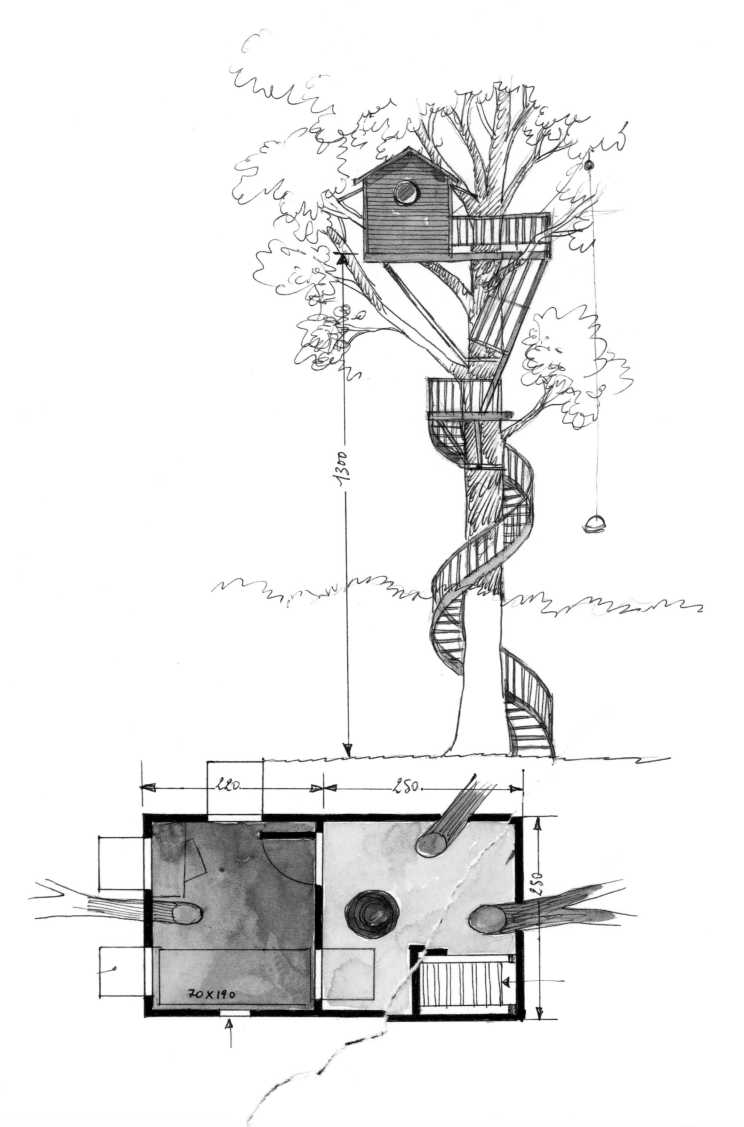

Originally, an extra deck was planned to the right of the treehouse, but since we are always very careful never to run the slightest risk, we decided to eliminate it. This pine leans at a rather steep angle, and we minimized the stress on it by placing most of the weight at the tree's center of gravity.

In the first version of this project, there were wooden props planned to support the platform upon which the treehouse rests, but to accentuate the effect of lightness, we eliminated all these props and suspended the platform entirely from nearly invisible cables.

Here, we're very high up! This treehouse fits within a fraction of an inch
between the branches of the great oak. No fewer than three large branches
pass through, as if the treehouse grew with the tree. On the roof a solar panel
provides illumination for the evening's reading.

This treehouse exemplifies all the challenges we've faced as designers. Imposing in size, it is built entirely onto this very large oak tree, complete with conveniences such as electricity and plumbing; yet all of the wiring and plumbing is concealed.

Independent of the trunk, there is a curved staircase that is almost freestanding. On the deck, there is a little round projection where you can eat breakfast.

To make the walkway as light as possible, we supported it on very slender pilings. In the end, this treehouse appears to float in space.

The client wanted this treehouse to be even more complex than what is drawn here. As a result, the roof was designed with multiple slopes, ridges, hips, and valleys that highlight the complexity of the project. Under the treehouse, there is a bathroom with concealed plumbing.

Notice the pretty hip roof that covers the entrance to this treehouse? The architecture of this treehouse is composed of elements that overlap with each other so as not to interfere with the character of the tree's branches.

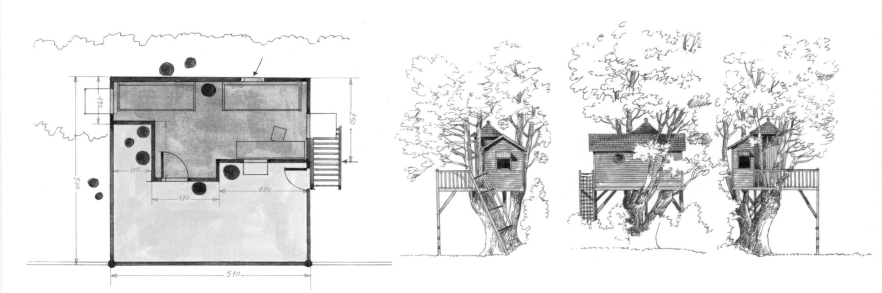

We sometimes use metal doors, windows, and bay windows in order to open the treehouse up as much as possible to nature, as seen in this example set in a beautiful walnut tree. The round columns of the treehouse harmonize with the central support of the spiral staircase.

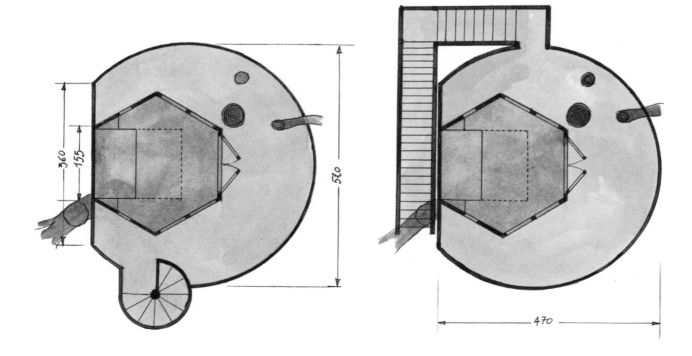

The spiral staircases we build are very popular with our clients. When the tree allows it, the result is always magnificent. Here, the initial design featured a straight stairway that extended directly from the ground. It took a lot of ingenuity and precision on the part of the builders to eventually thread the stairway through the branches and make it climb up the tree completely in a spiral.

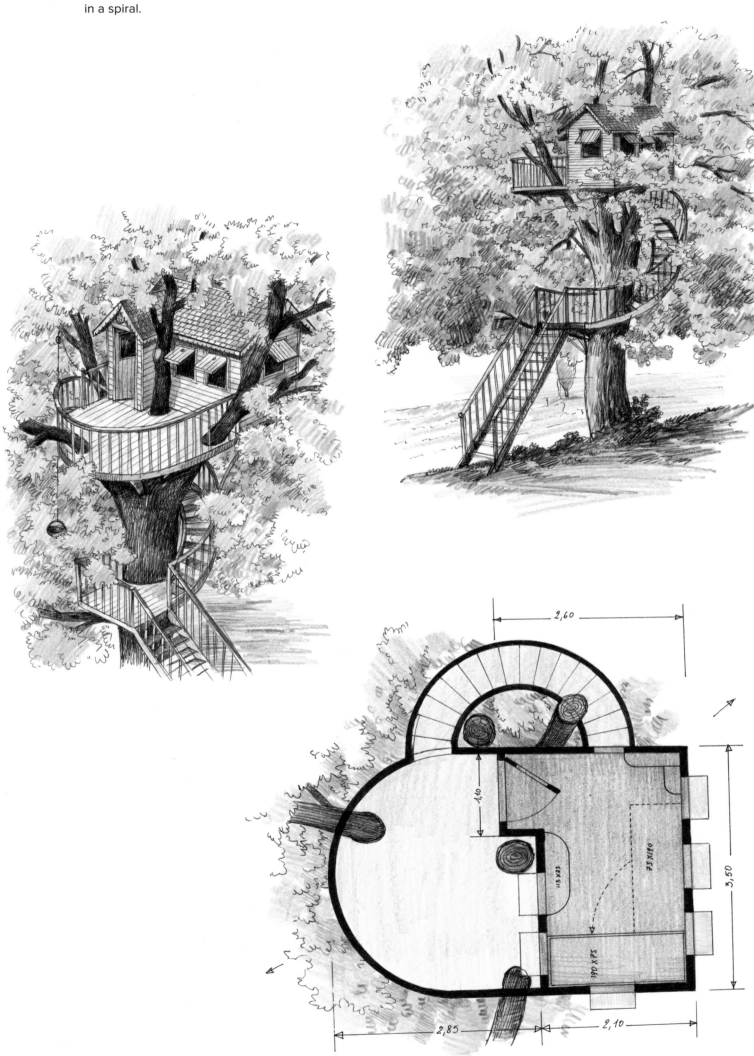

The initial design was later modified with our client. The entrance to the treehouse is through a hanging walkway that extends from the sloping ground. This is another example of a treehouse that is well integrated into the tree that supports it.

It is rare for us to build a cabin on the ground, but we can never refuse our friend Dominique Lafourcade, a very talented landscape artist. Under her supervision we constructed a cabin out of bamboo. In the photos you can see the level of detail and workmanship that was invested in the interior decoration and the charming curve of the roof.

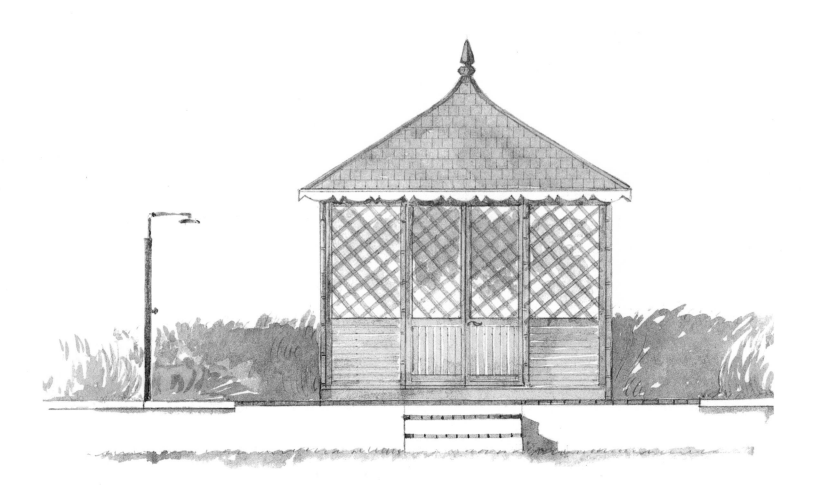

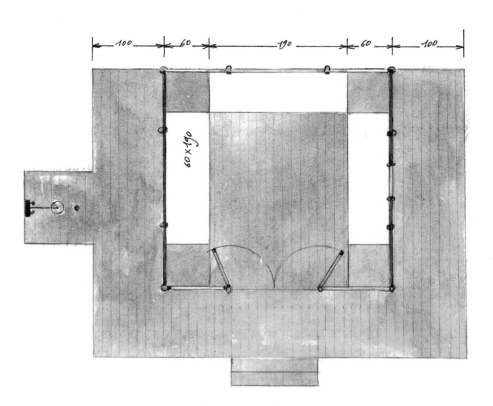

This treehouse is built between two great oaks, and its spiral staircase acts as a third support. Thus, the load is divided between the triangle of the two trees and the central column of the staircase.

TREEHOUSE 15 ___
(PAGE 94)

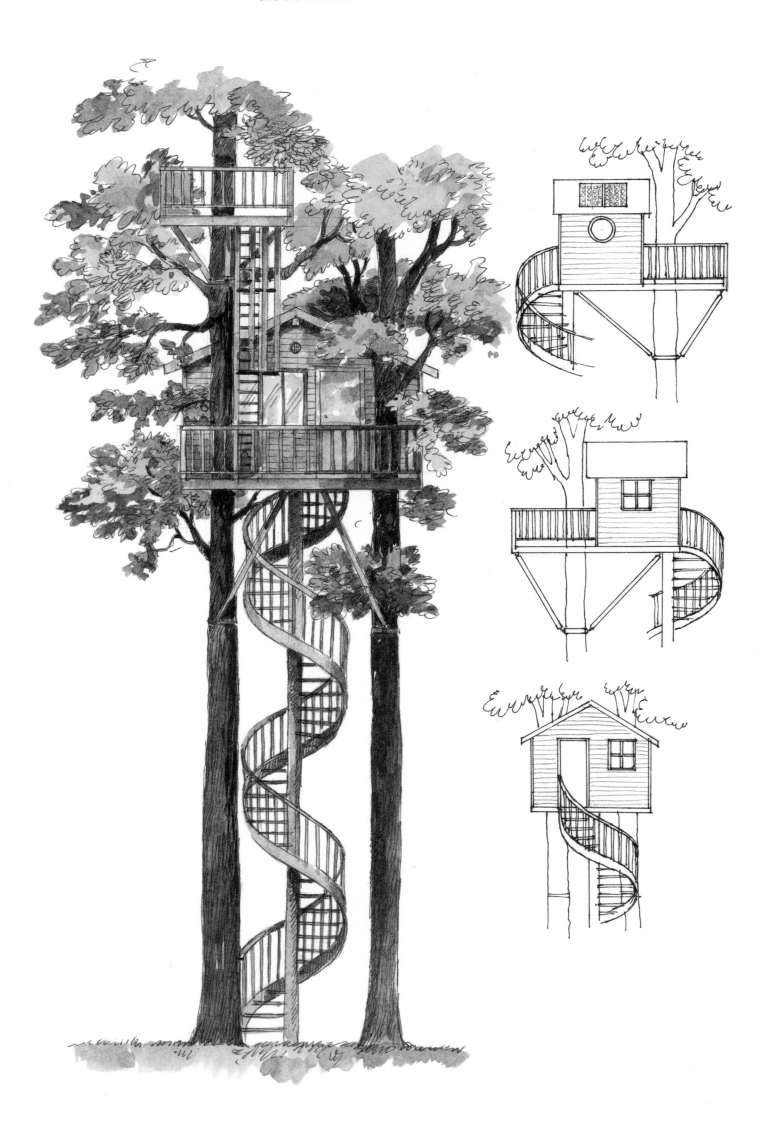

The platform of this floating pagoda is almost 1,100 square feet, and the cabin 240 square feet. In other words, it felt as if we were building an ocean liner! The interior timberwork is a hammer-beam truss. Note the complexity of the roof's shape; it is covered with tiles of lacquered metal. The interior was crafted with particular care by our carpenters to give the entire cabin a tranquil feeling.

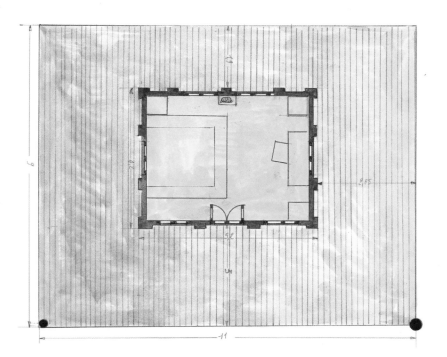

Two great oaks shelter this treehouse. One carries the bulk of the weight of the treehouse, the other that of the deck. Thus, the whole treehouse has reasonable proportions and is very well integrated. A patio and walkway encircle the treehouse and give access to the spectacular views. The interior features a sofa bed and a series of furniture pieces made by our craftsmen.

You can see in the photos that this treehouse is a jewel, with many finishing touches that accentuate its Asian design. Its sliding doors open wide into nature. Its handrails, its very steeply sloping roof, and the casing of its windows were all created to transport you.

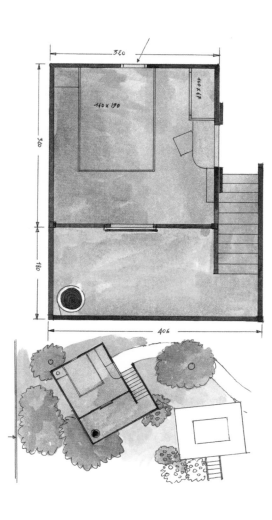

Here again, the tree's branches interfered with the original layout of the staircase, so we created three staircases in one: straight, curved, and spiral.

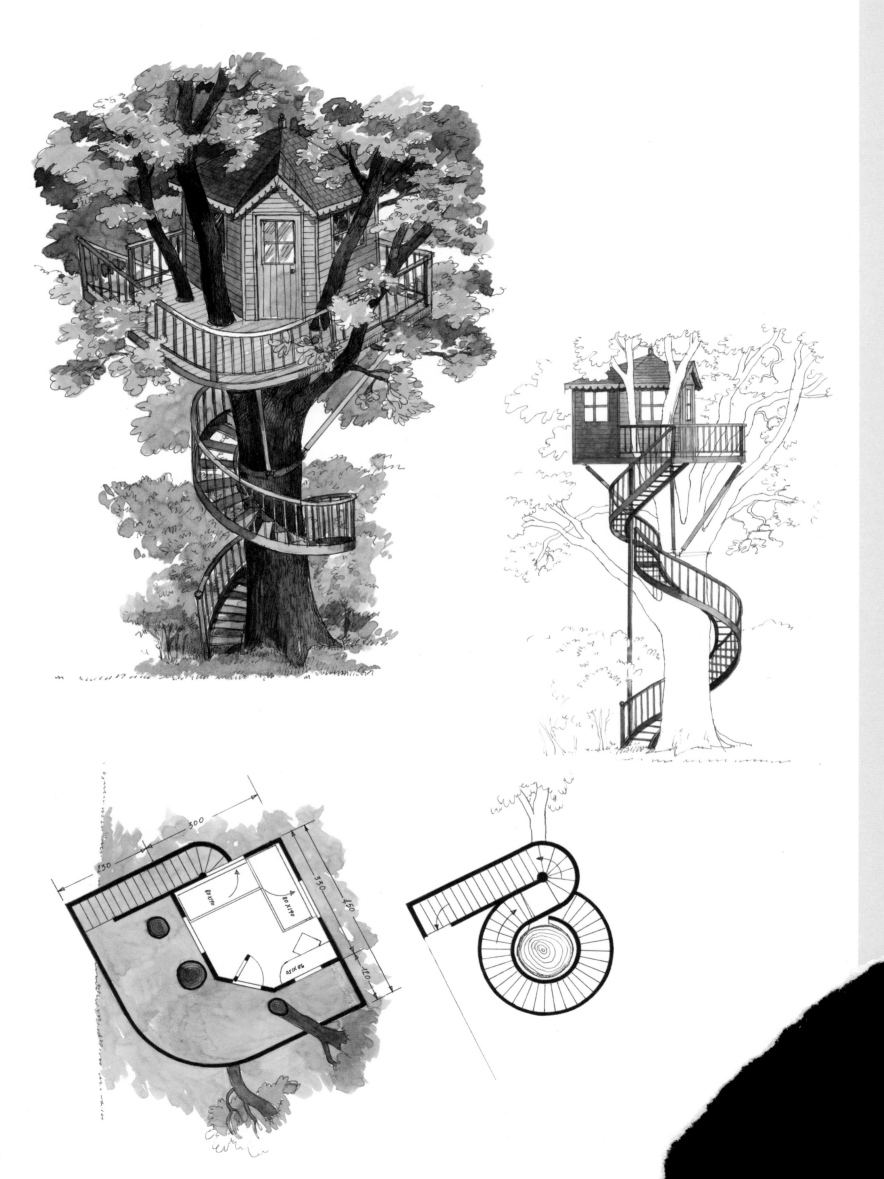

At forty-three feet this is the tallest spiral staircase we've ever built. It leads directly to the deck. The treehouse is spacious and open to the sea.

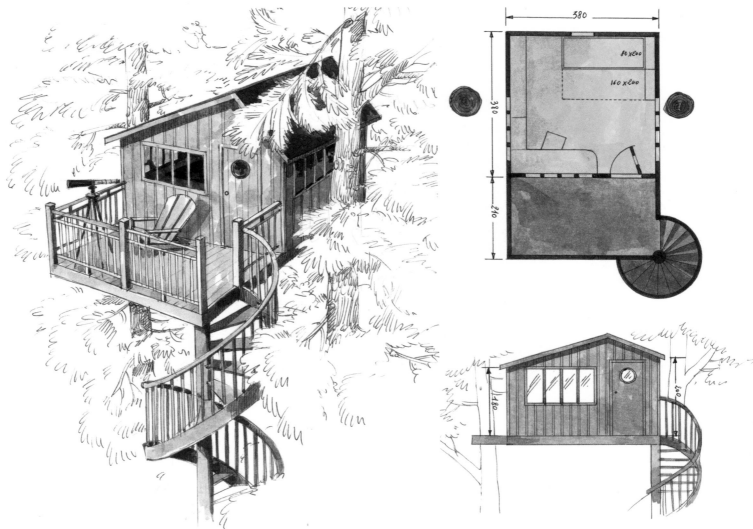

Our House on the Water, built of red cedar is replete with luxuries. It is completely isolated, and its roof is covered with wooden shingles. Its floats are built by a leading specialist. The living room is fully furnished, and the cabin is equipped with a gas stove. There is a miniature bathroom with a dry toilet and a demijohn of drinking water for brushing your teeth, oil lamps for lighting.

These pines weren't enormous, but the treehouse and its deck are substantial. We planted columns discretely between the trees. When you're up above, you get the impression that there's nothing beneath your feet.

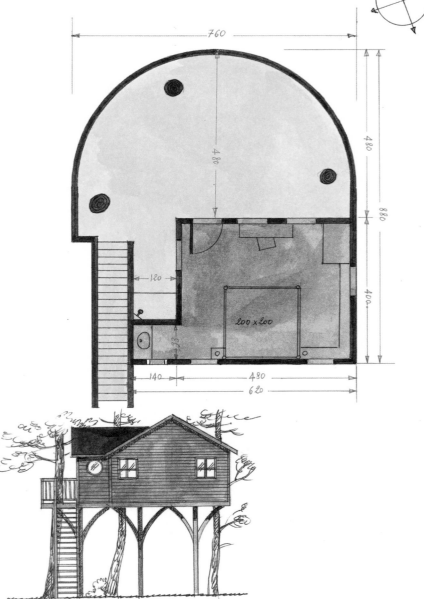

This tree was born to receive a treehouse. The space where we placed it was waiting for us. Not a single branch in our way: a dream!

This treehouse was built between two distant trees, and yet it has no additional support. We imagined a very long reinforcing beam—half wood, half steel—in order to span the very long distance.

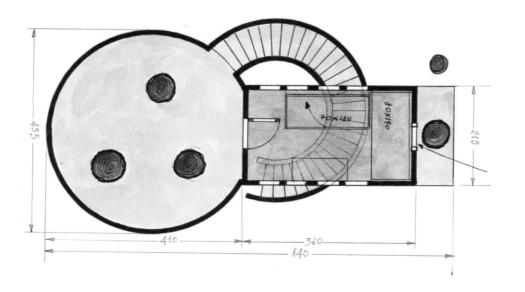

This is nothing but a thicket of small oaks, yet the treehouse seems to float upon them without weighing them down. Here we chose large metal picture windows to open the treehouse as much as possible to the panoramic view.

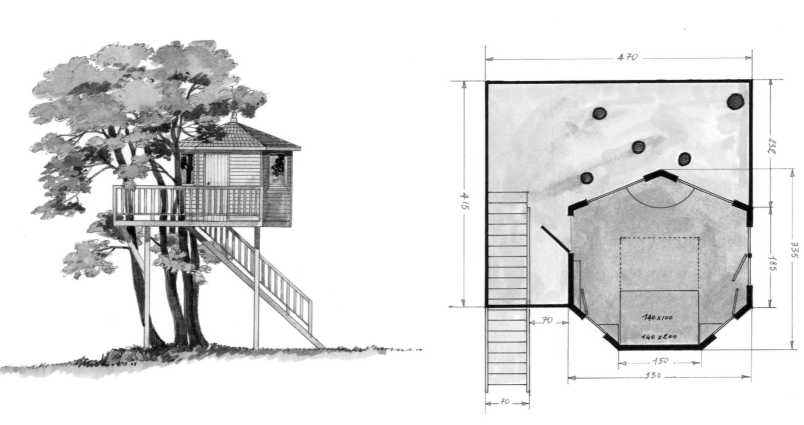

Here we took on a monster: an immense redwood. We had to find the right proportions for the treehouse and enlarge the supports, particularly the metal pieces of the crown that receive the tie beams. Note the charm of the circular bench that rings the trunk. The initial three flights of stairs took up too much space, so we finally decided on a spiral staircase.

The staircase unrolls around a neighboring tree, climbs, and arrives at a walkway suspended between two trees. From this walkway you reach the round deck. The treehouse is built between three trees. This project is a good example of the use of space and overlapping trees.

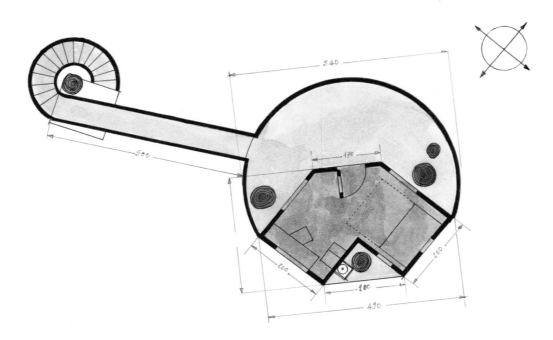

This great oak has always been inhabited. There had been an old treehouse—respectable, but rotten. We removed it and refurbished the tree. Note the number of branches we had to avoid in the deck.

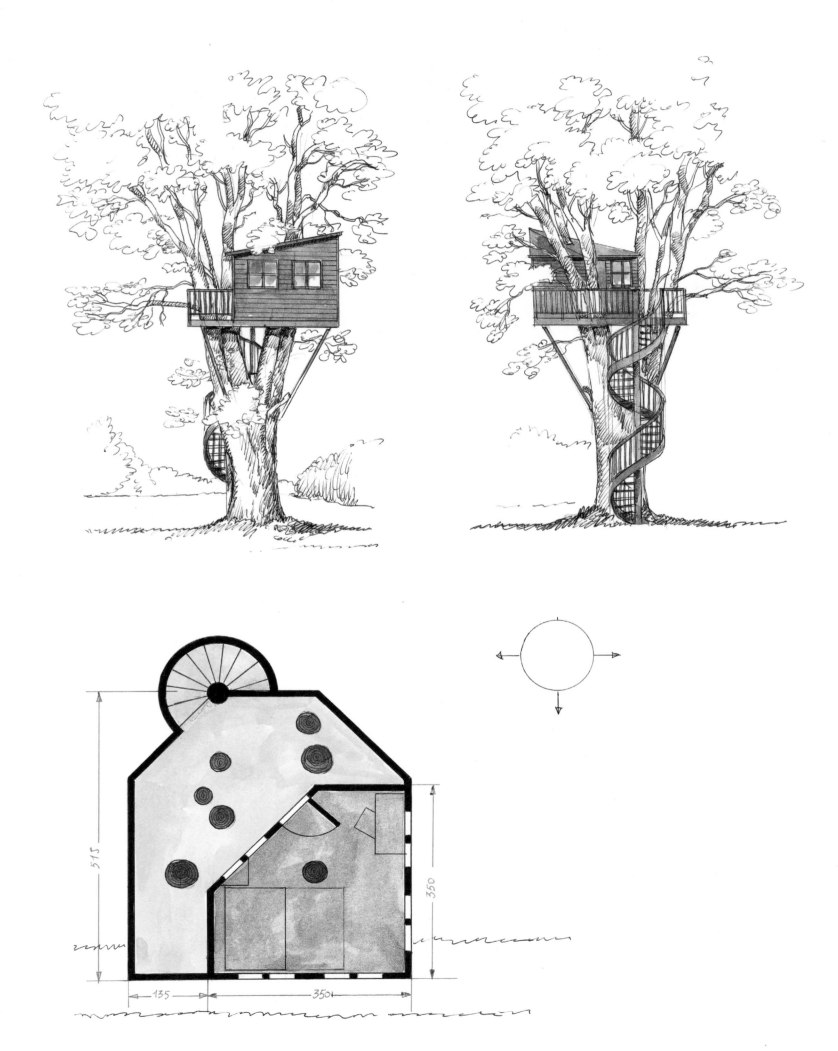

The immense beech tree renders this large guesthouse nearly invisible. The guesthouse can be reached by a large staircase with two flights, then a walkway that extends across the park. The bathroom is installed under the treehouse, with none of the plumbing visible.

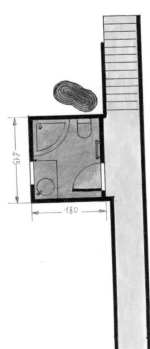

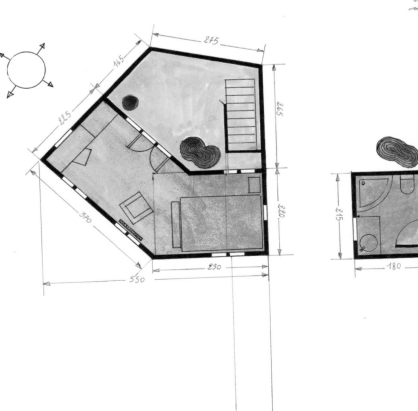